DISNEY MOVIE CLASSICS

FIVE FINGER PIANO

- 2 **BABY MINE**
  Dumbo

- 8 **BELLE**
  Beauty and the Beast

- 5 **DALMATIAN PLANTATION**
  101 Dalmatians

- 12 **HE'S A PIRATE**
  Pirates of the Caribbean

- 17 **ONCE UPON A DREAM**
  Sleeping Beauty

- 20 **PART OF YOUR WORLD**
  The Little Mermaid

- 30 **SCALES AND ARPEGGIOS**
  The Aristocats

- 26 **TOUCH THE SKY**
  Brave

ISBN 978-1-4803-6320-5

Disney characters and artwork © Disney Enterprises, Inc.

Walt Disney Music Company
Wonderland Music Company, Inc.

DISTRIBUTED BY

7777 W. BLUEMOUND RD. P.O. BOX 13819 MILWAUKEE, WI 53213

For all works contained herein:
Unauthorized copying, arranging, adapting, recording, Internet posting, public performance,
or other distribution of the printed music in this publication is an infringement of copyright.
Infringers are liable under the law.

Visit Hal Leonard Online at
www.halleonard.com

Baby Mine
from Walt Disney's DUMBO

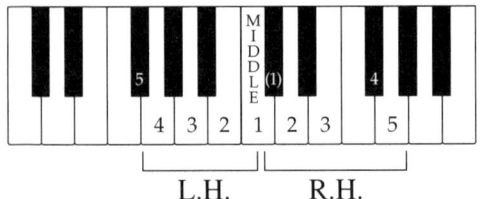

Words by Ned Washington
Music by Frank Churchill

Duet Part (Student plays one octave higher than written.)

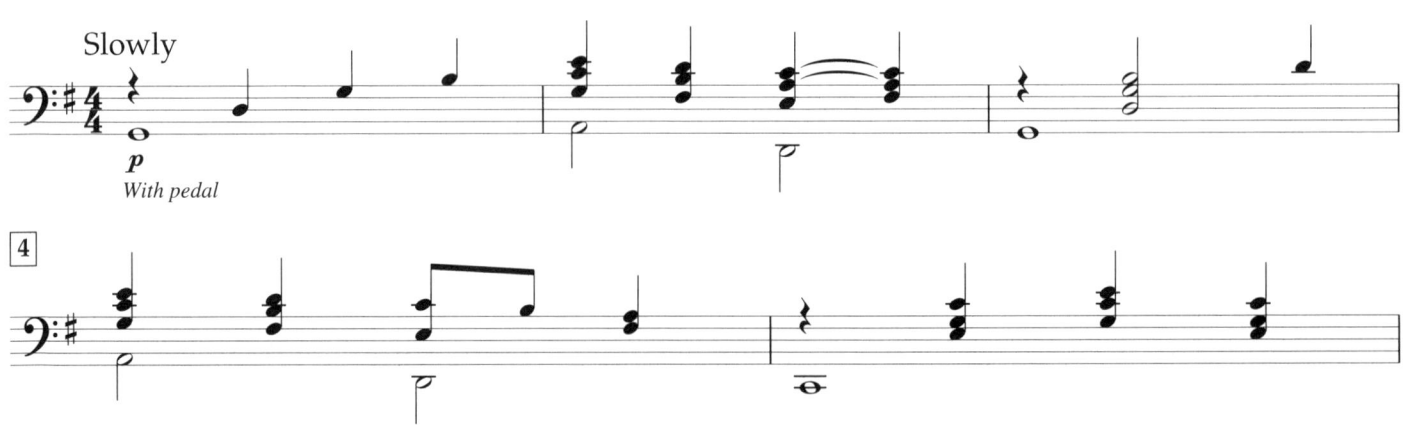

Copyright © 1941 by Walt Disney Productions
Copyright Renewed
World Rights Controlled by Bourne Co. (ASCAP)
International Copyright Secured   All Rights Reserved

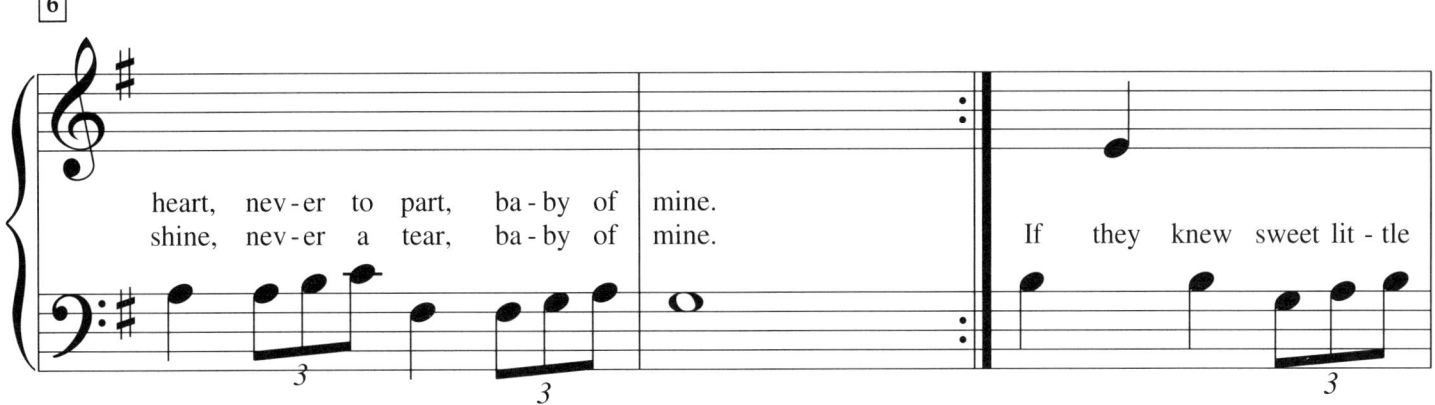

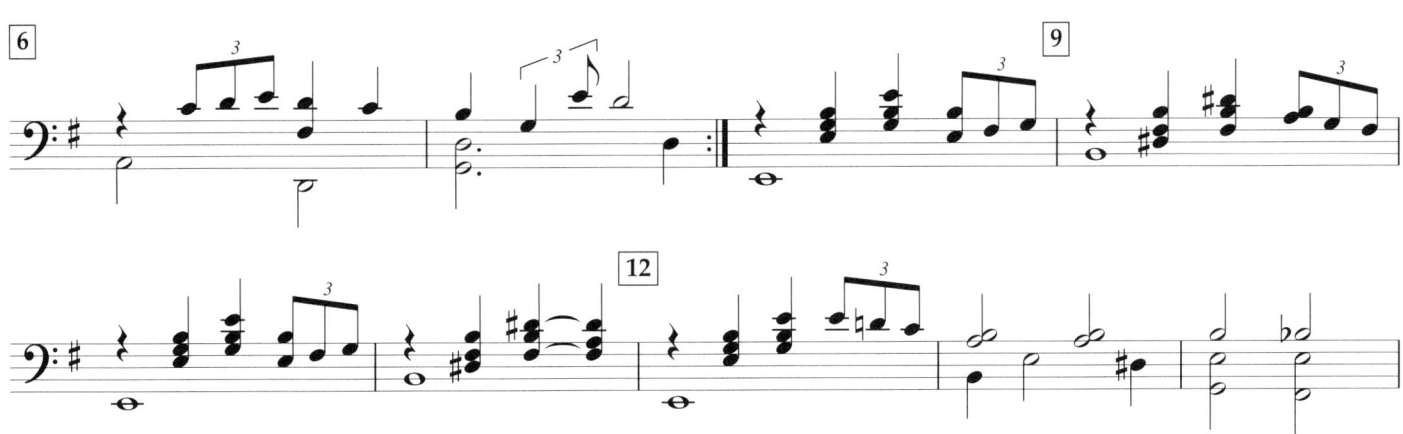

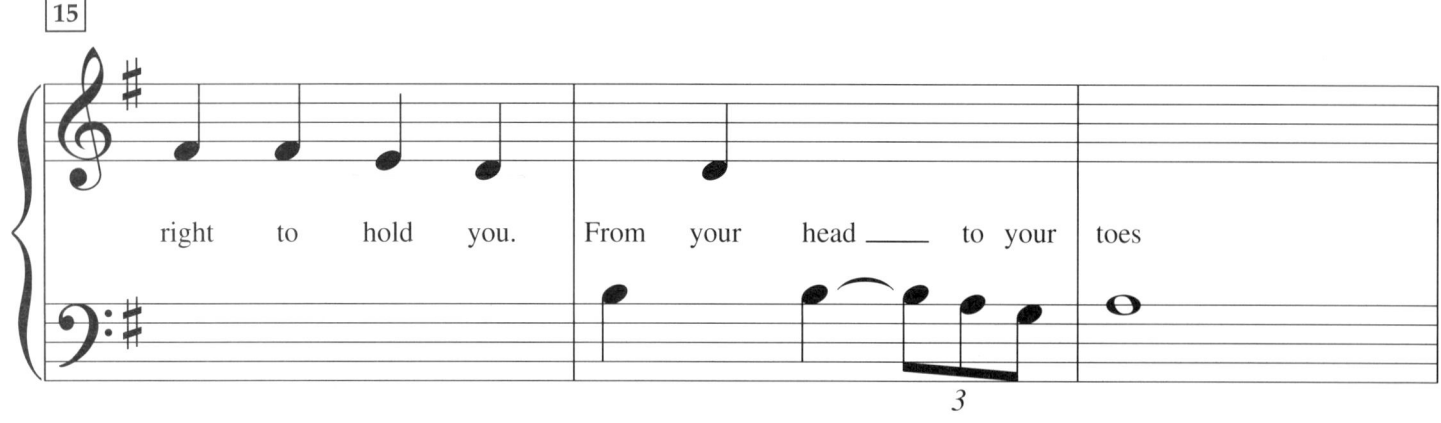
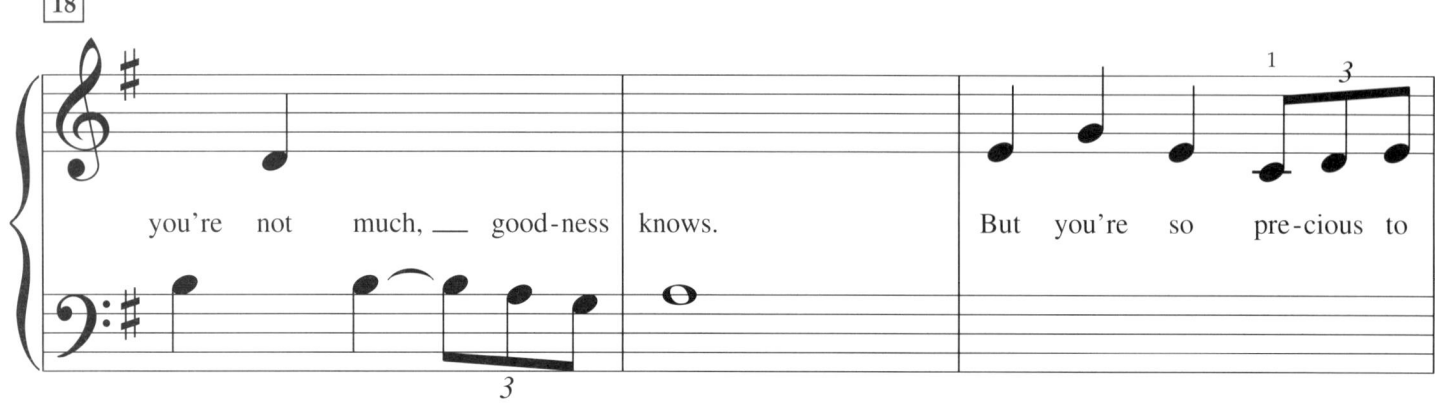
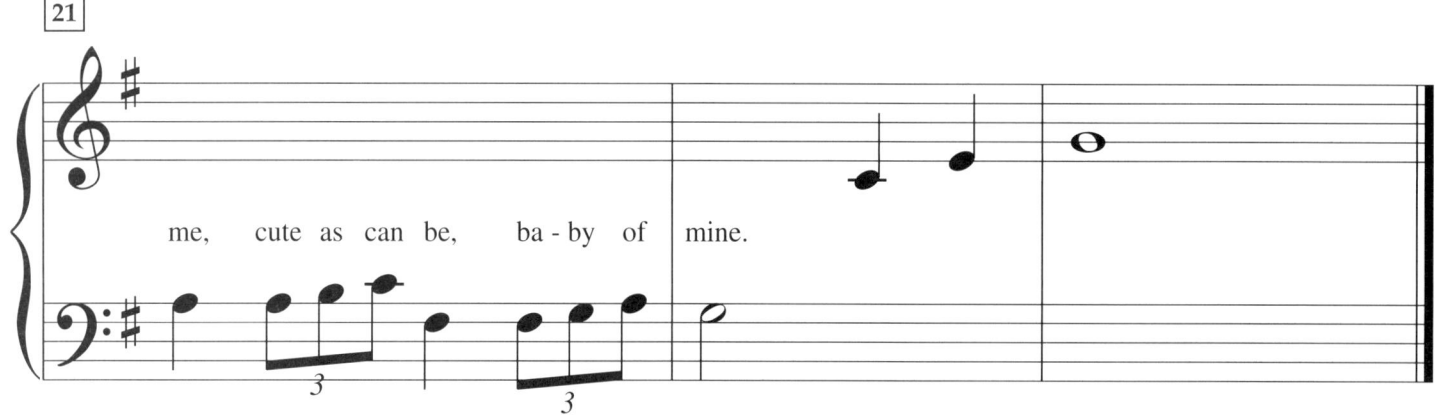

Dalmatian Plantation
from Walt Disney's 101 DALMATIANS

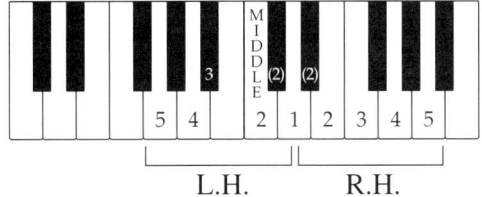

Words and Music by
Mel Leven

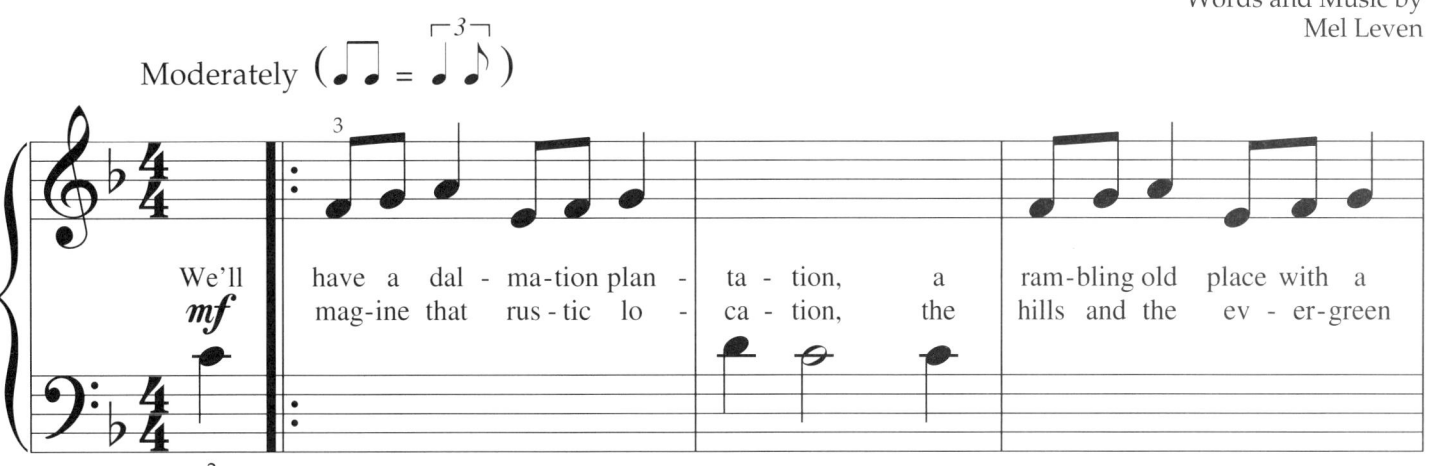

Duet Part (Student plays one octave higher than written.)

© 1959 Walt Disney Music Company
Copyright Renewed
All Rights Reserved   Used by Permission

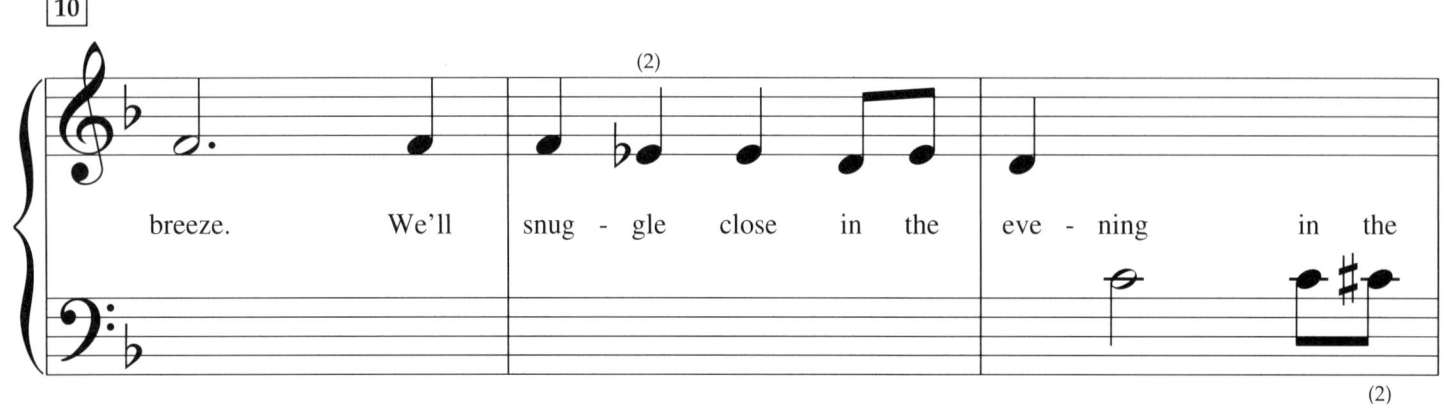

Belle
from Walt Disney's BEAUTY AND THE BEAST

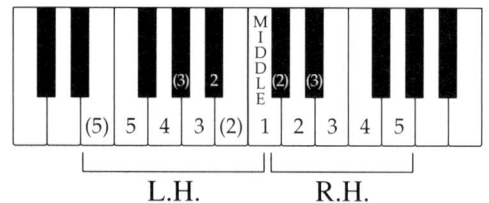

Lyrics by Howard Ashman
Music by Alan Menken

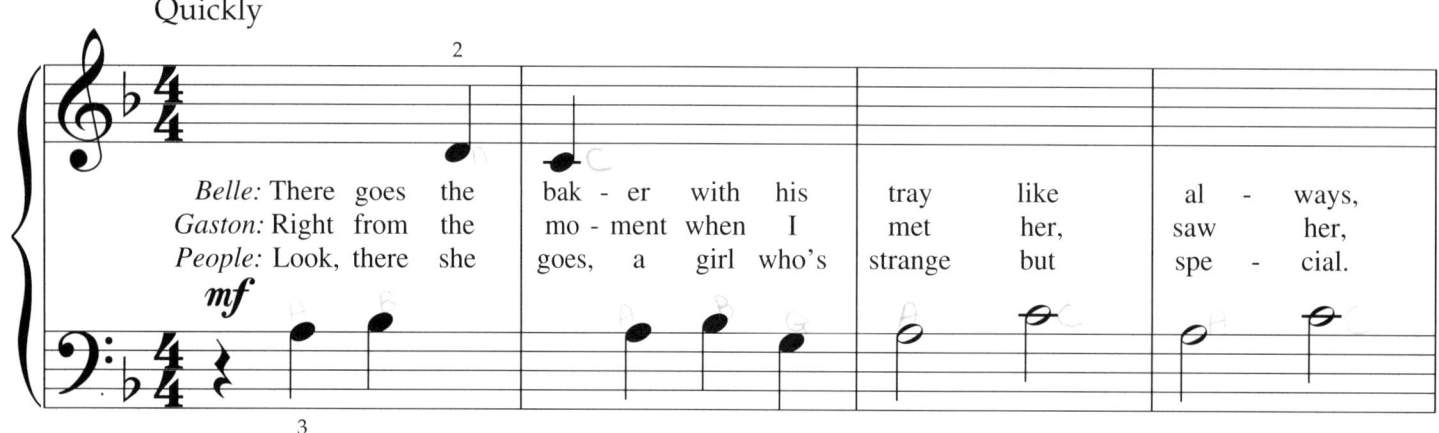

Duet Part (Student plays one octave higher than written.)

© 1991 Walt Disney Music Company and Wonderland Music Company, Inc.
All Rights Reserved   Used by Permission

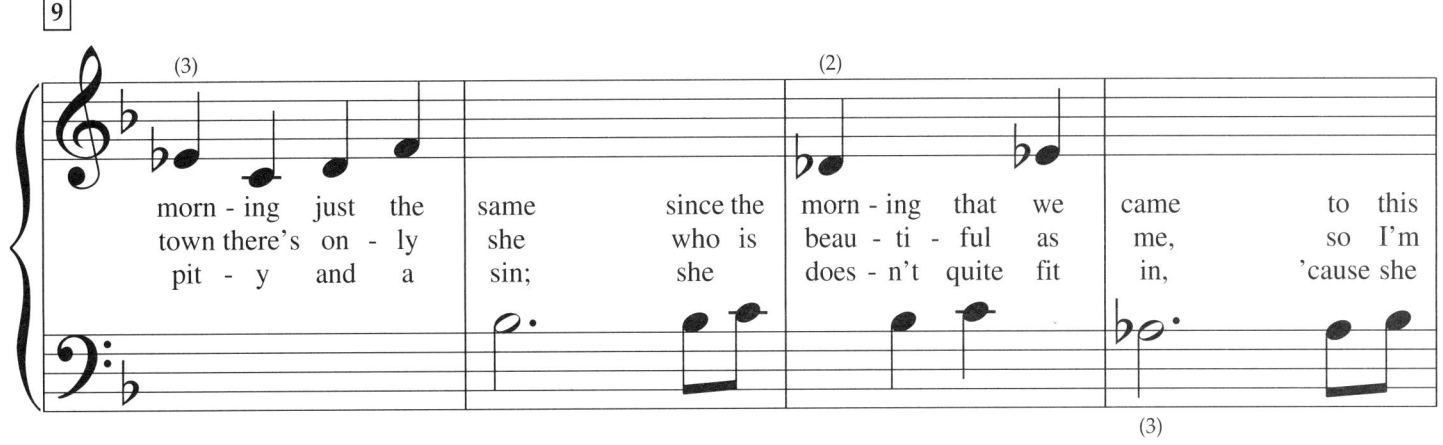

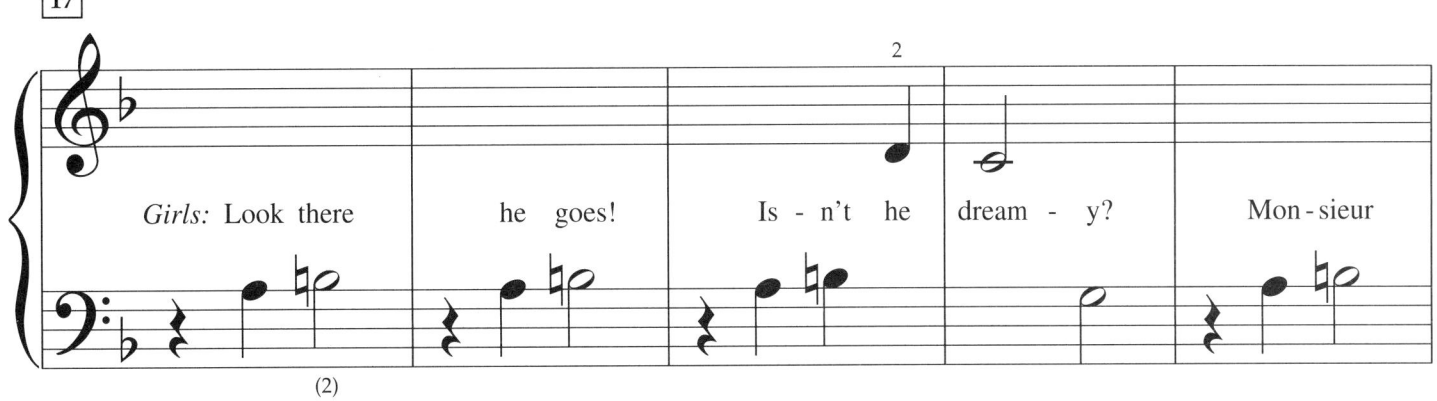

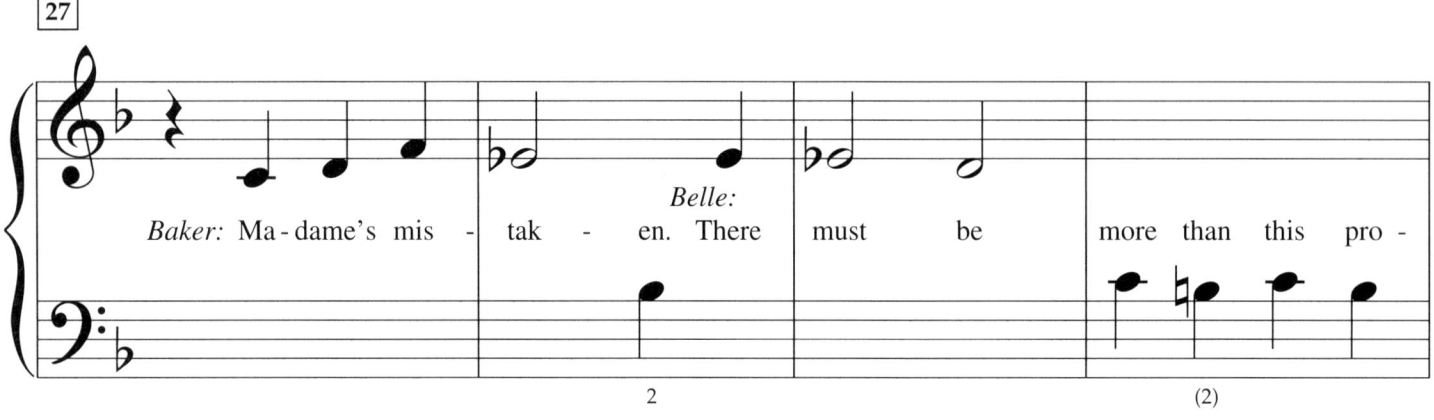

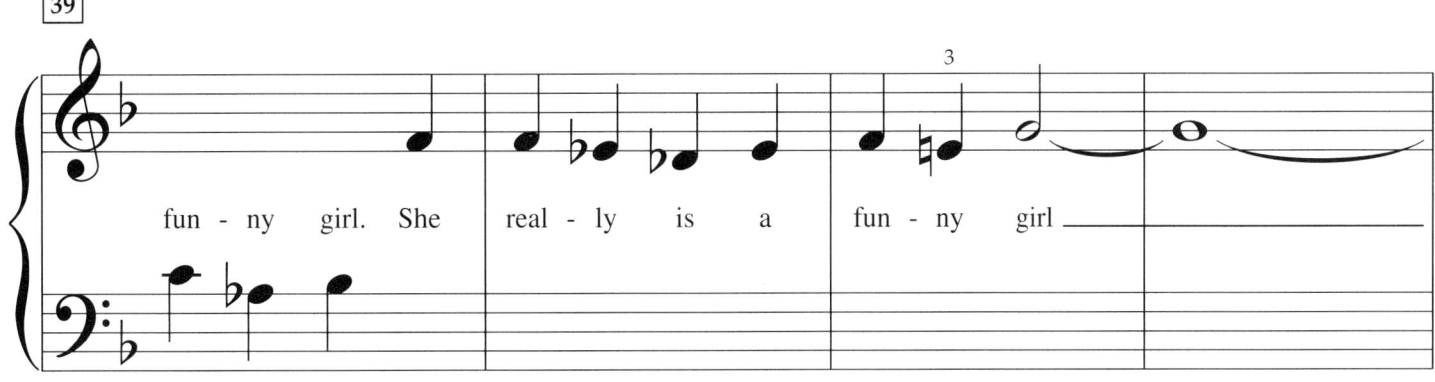
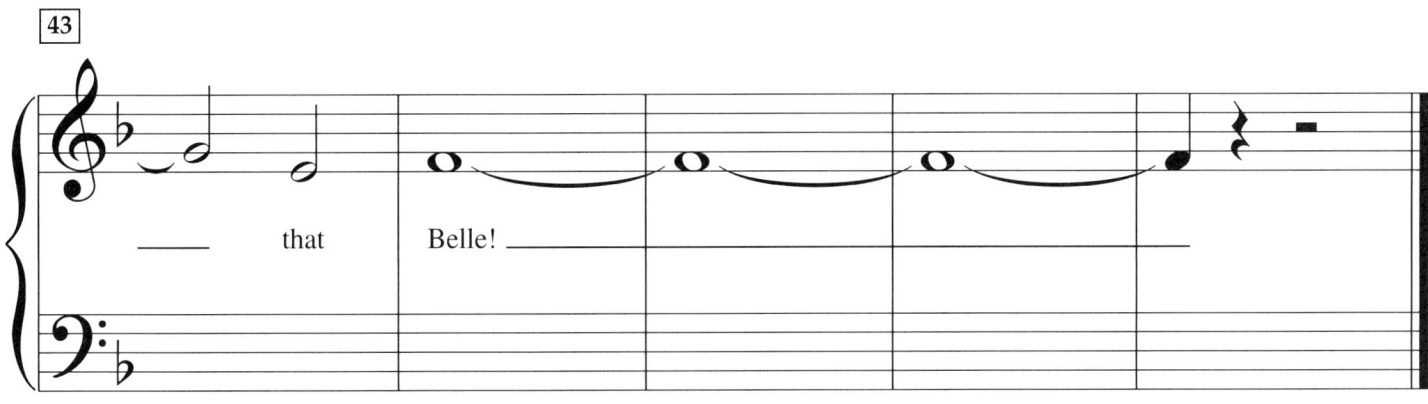
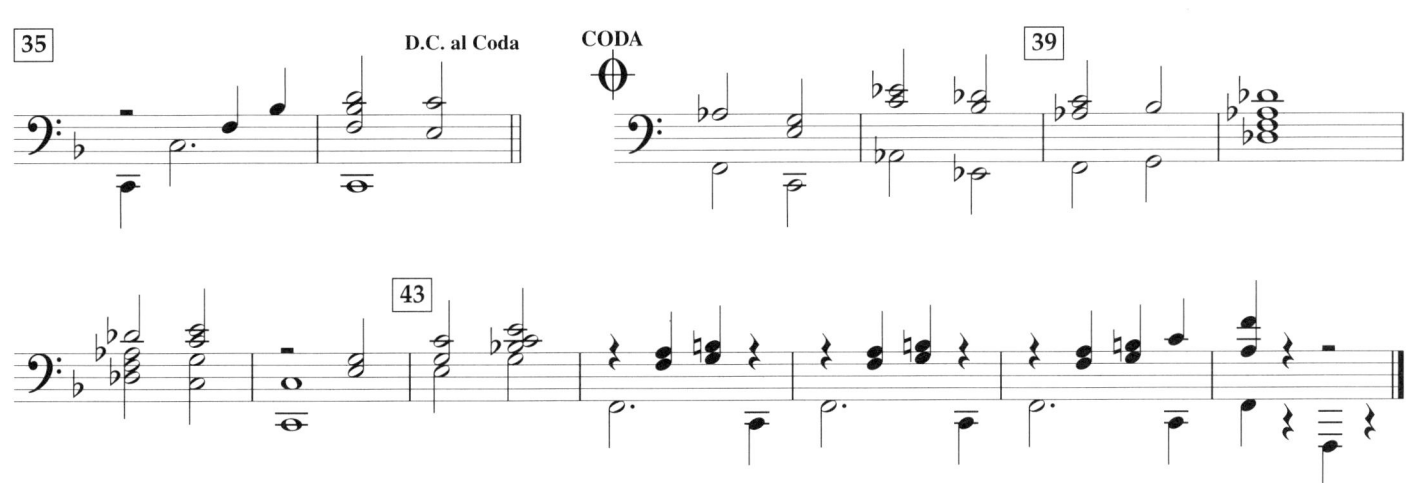

He's a Pirate
from Walt Disney Pictures' PIRATES OF THE CARIBBEAN: THE CURSE OF THE BLACK PEARL

Music by Klaus Badelt

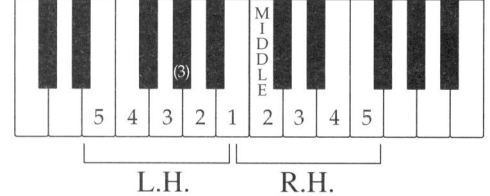

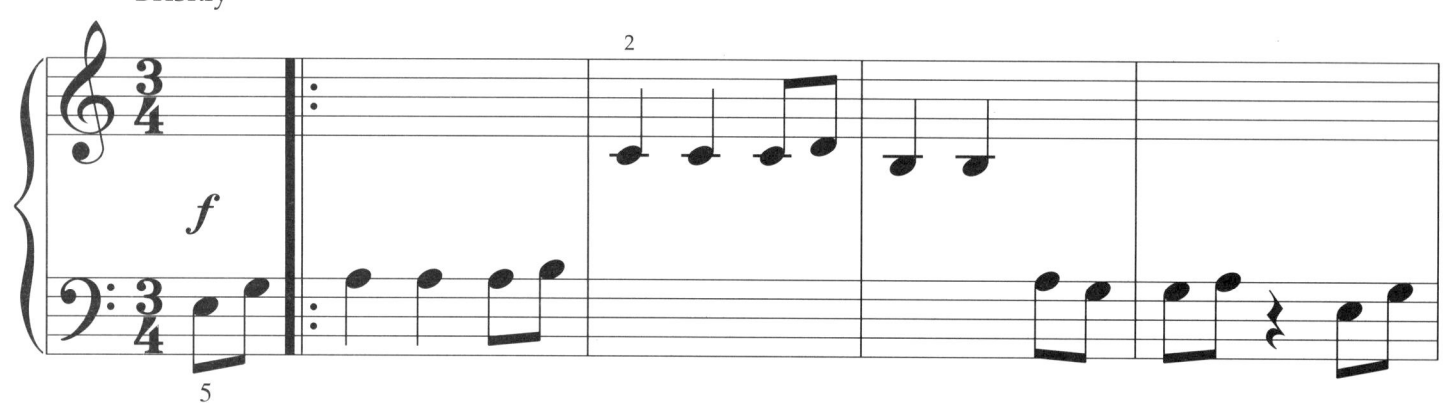

Duet Part (Student plays one octave higher than written.)

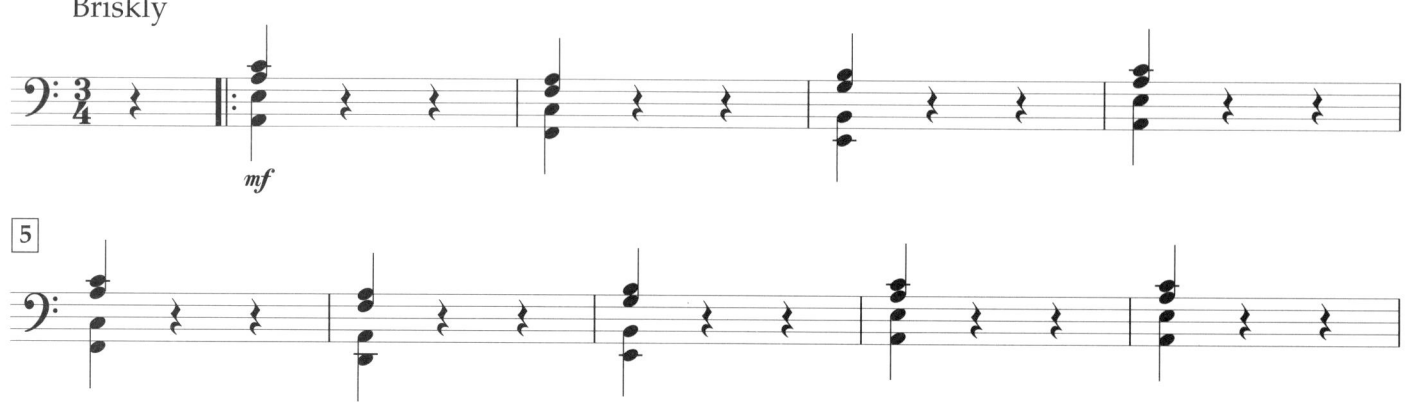

© 2003 Walt Disney Music Company
All Rights Reserved   Used by Permission

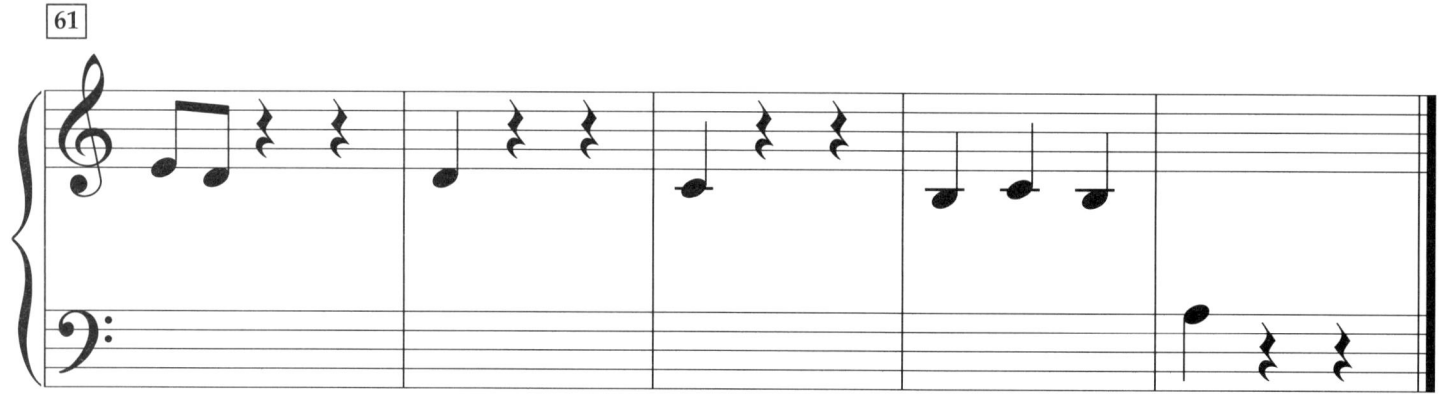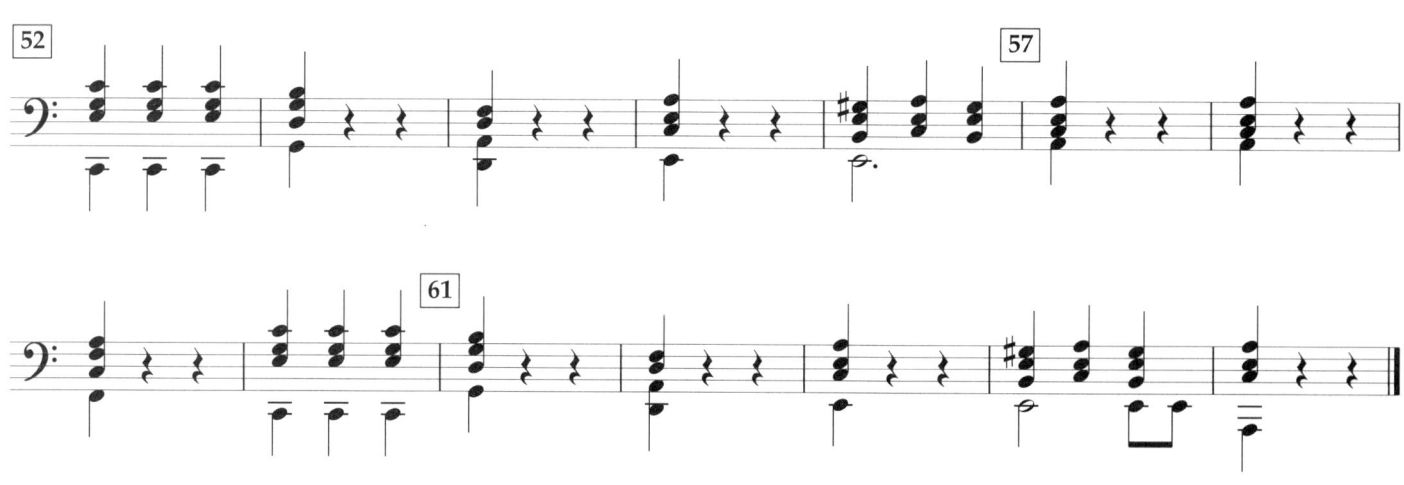

Once Upon a Dream
from Walt Disney's SLEEPING BEAUTY

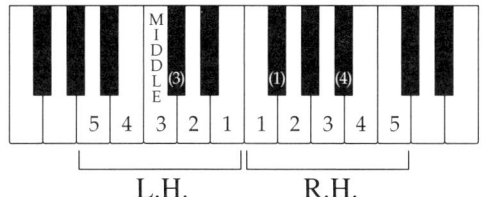

Words and Music by Sammy Fain
and Jack Lawrence
Adapted from a Theme by Tchaikovsky

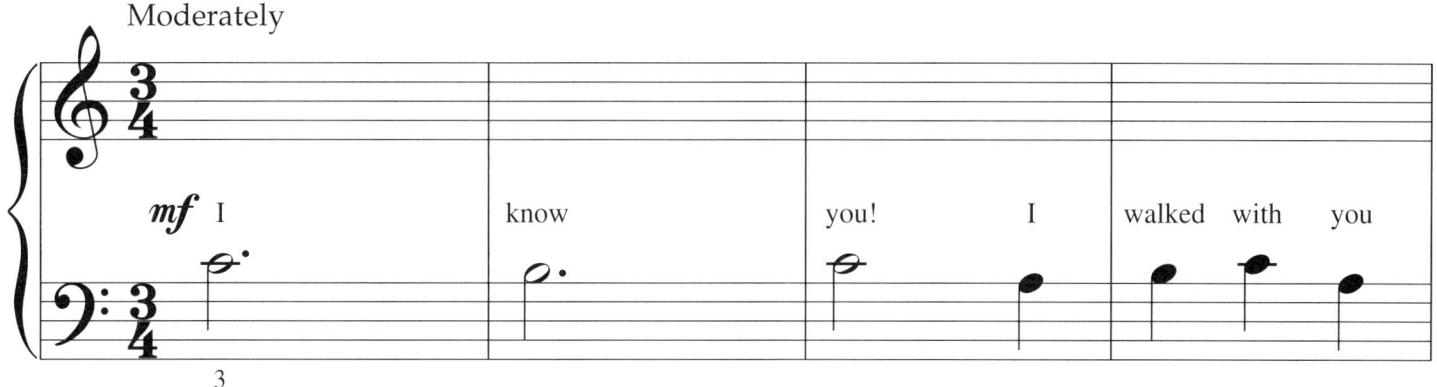

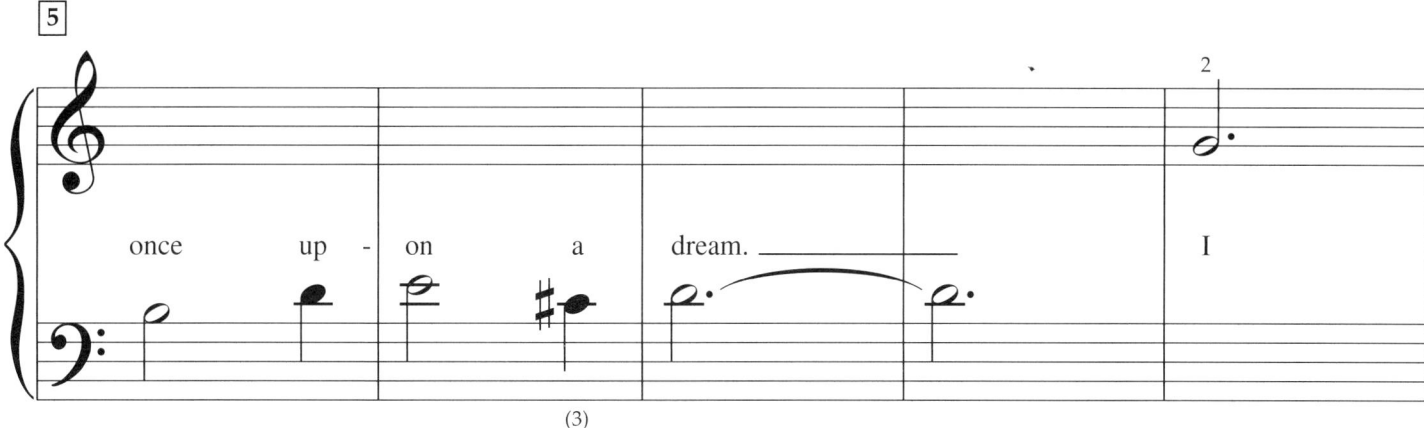

Duet Part (Student plays one octave higher than written.)

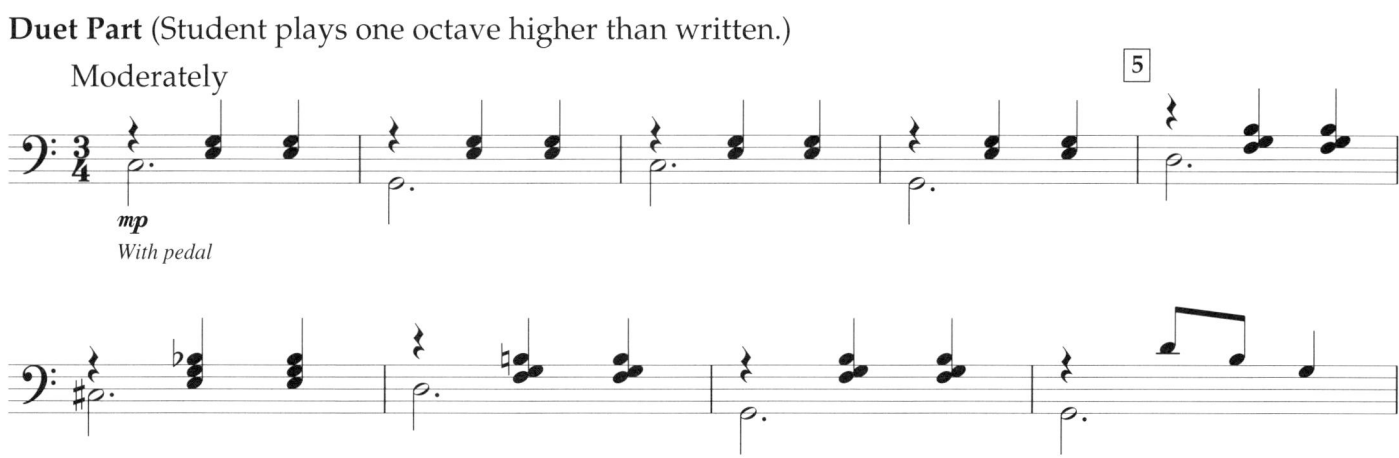

© 1952 Walt Disney Music Company
Copyright Renewed
All Rights Reserved   Used by Permission

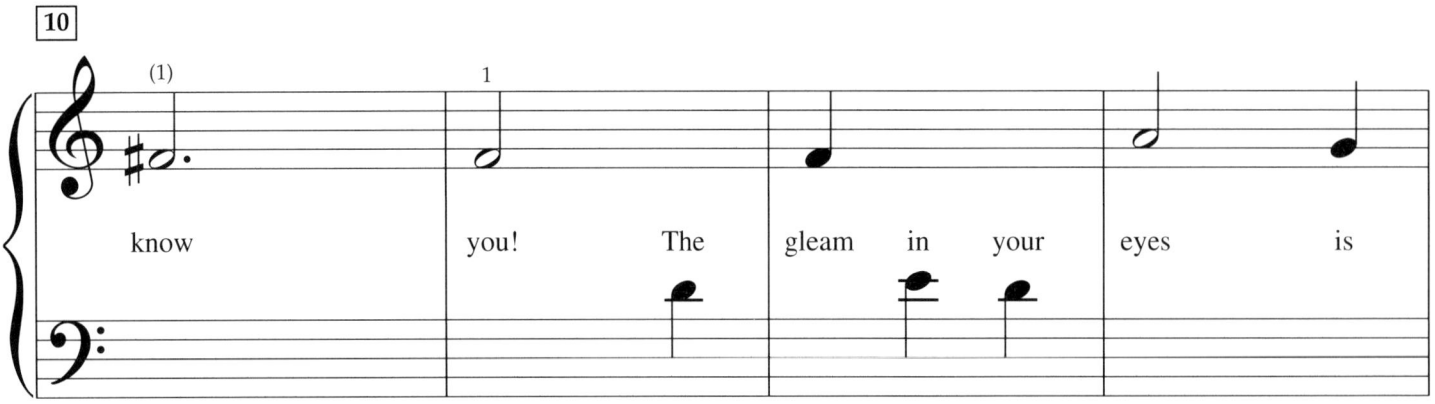
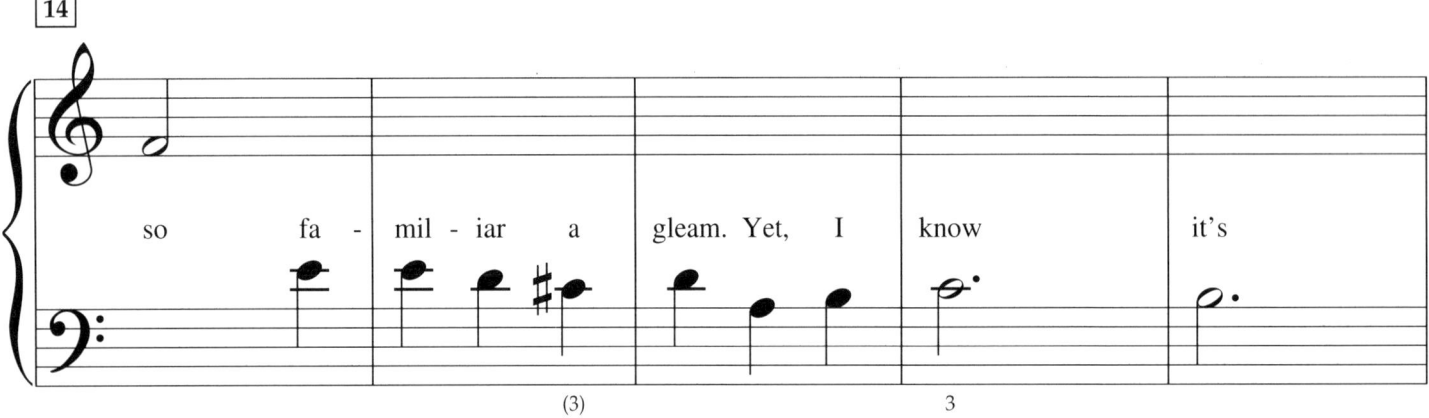
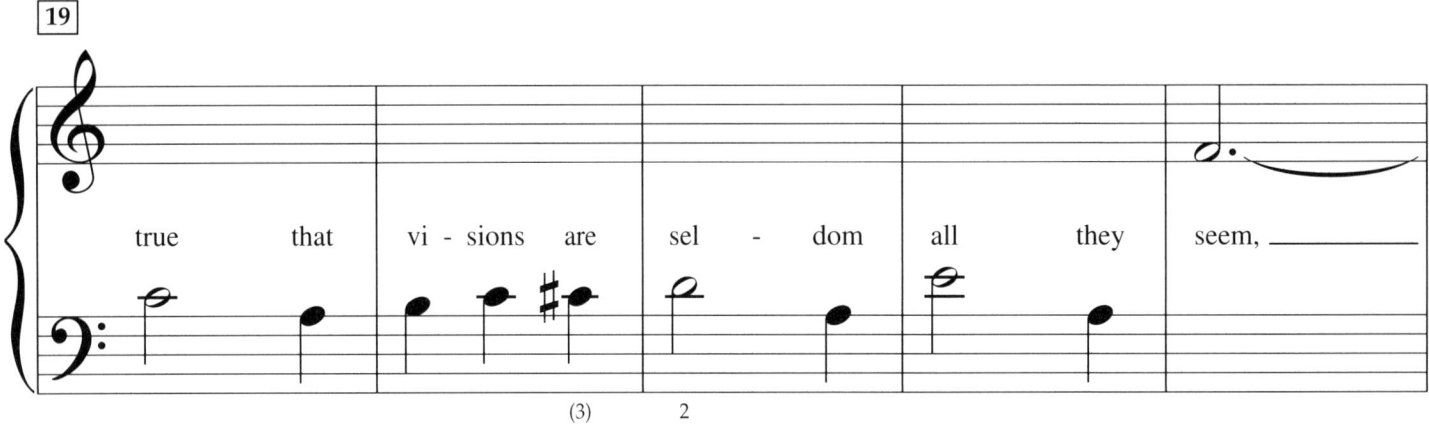

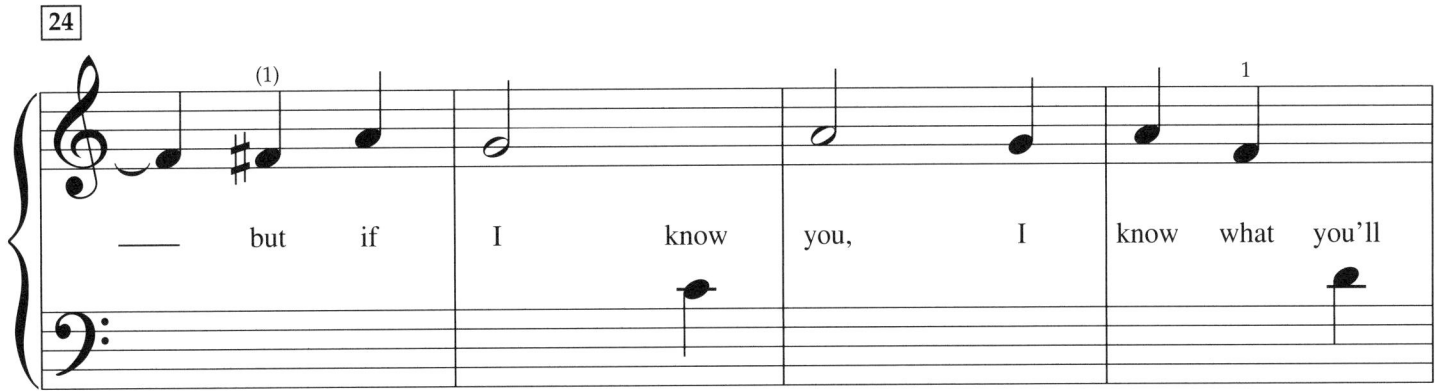
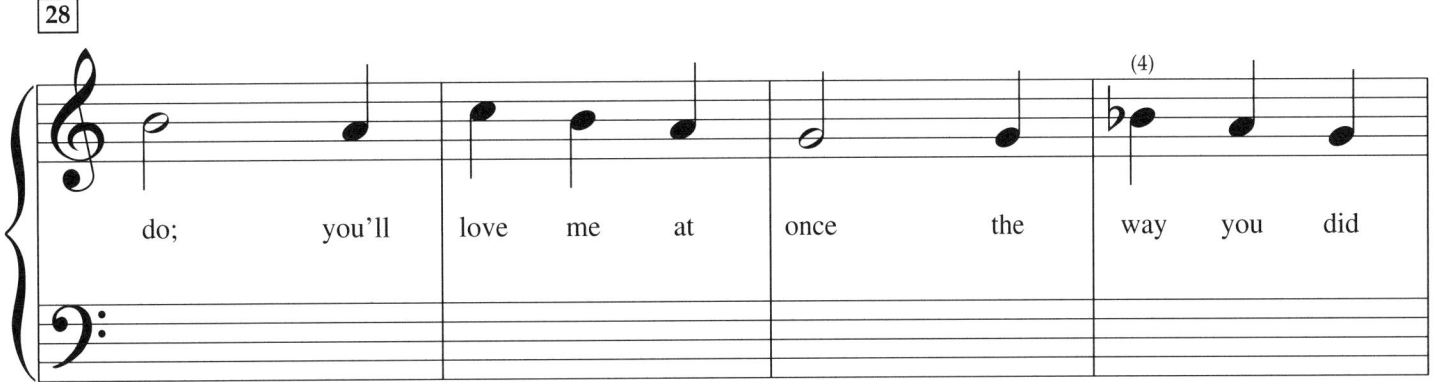
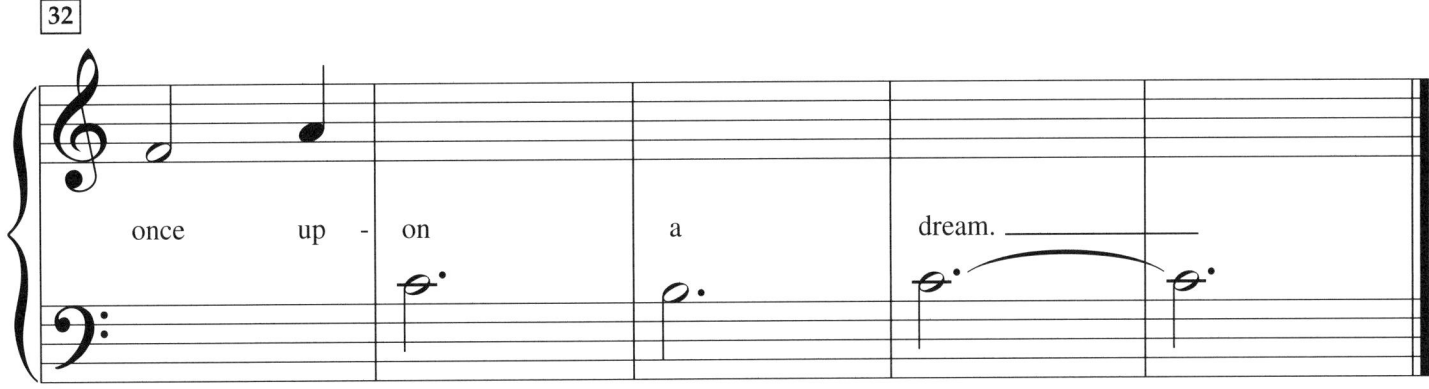

Part of Your World
from Walt Disney's THE LITTLE MERMAID

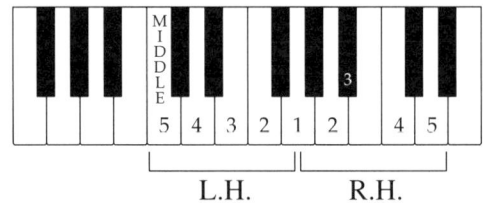

Music by Alan Menken
Lyrics by Howard Ashman

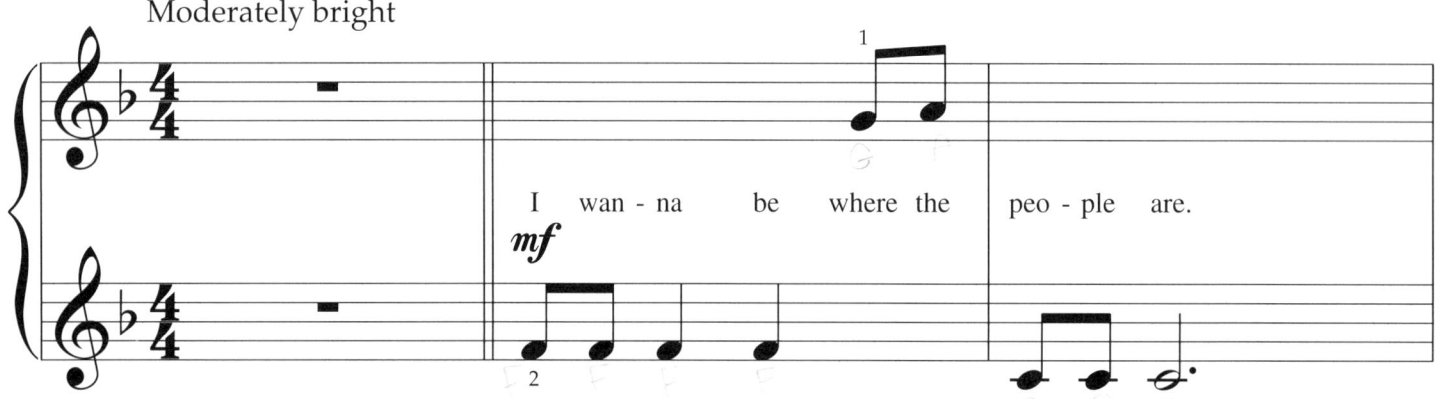

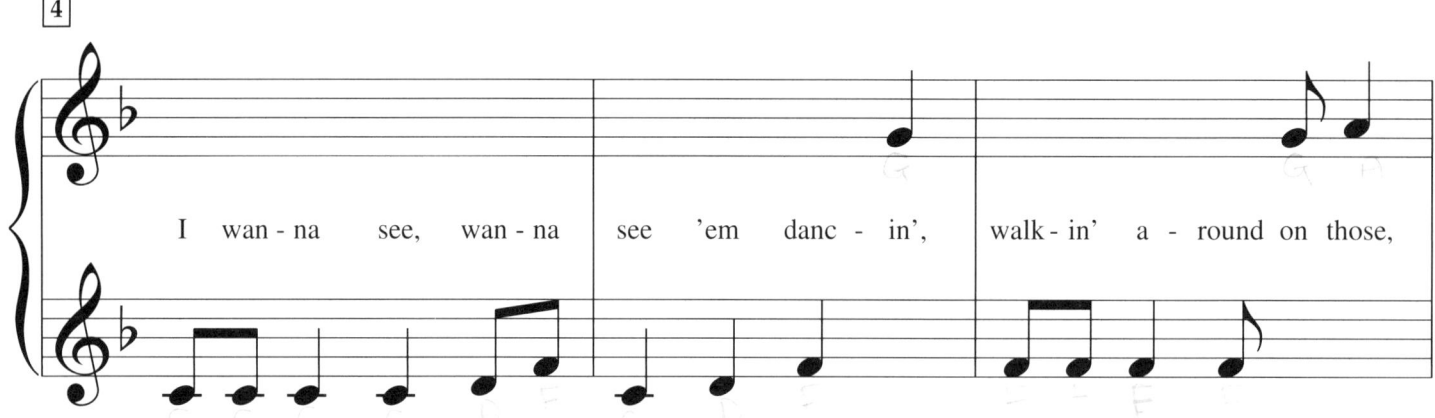

Duet Part (Student plays one octave higher than written.)

© 1988 Wonderland Music Company, Inc. and Walt Disney Music Company
All Rights Reserved   Used by Permission

Touch the Sky
from the Walt Disney/Pixar film BRAVE

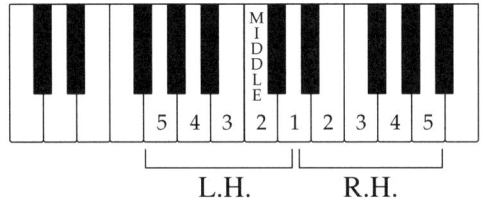

Music by Alexander L. Mandel
Lyrics by Alexander L. Mandel
and Mark Andrews

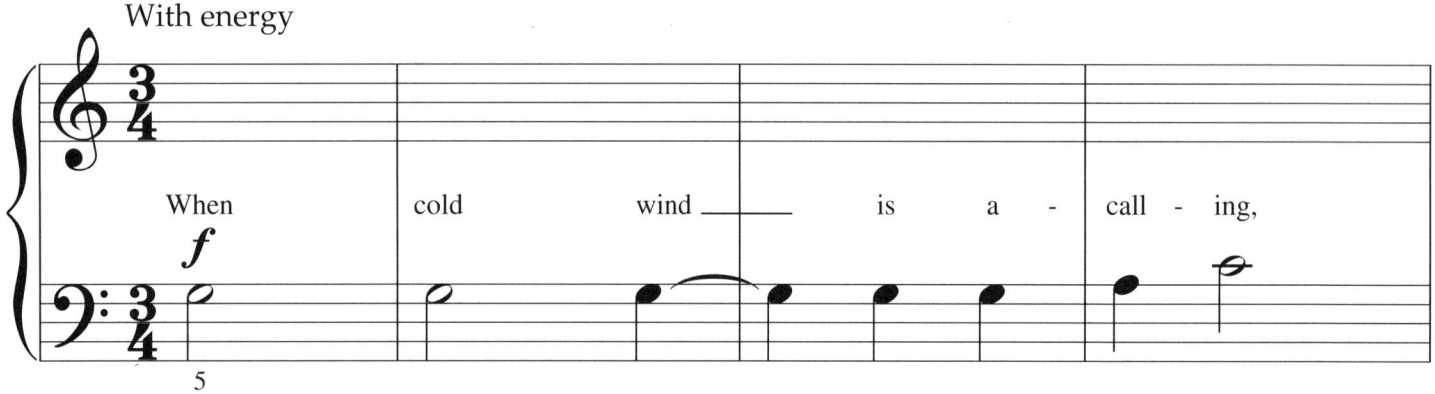

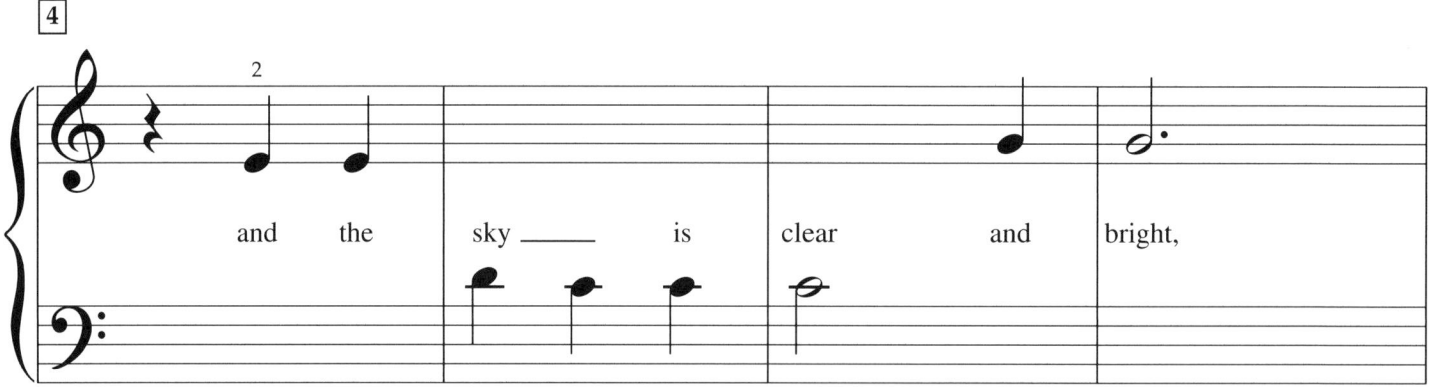

Duet Part (Student plays one octave higher than written.)

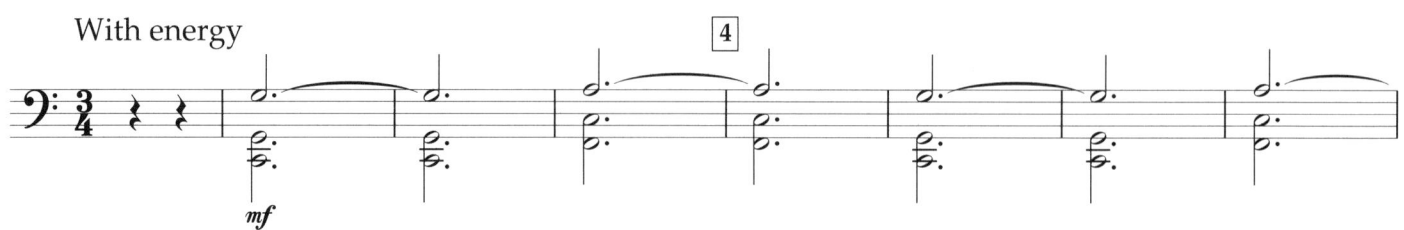

© 2012 Walt Disney Music Company and Pixar Talking Pictures
All Rights Reserved   Used by Permission

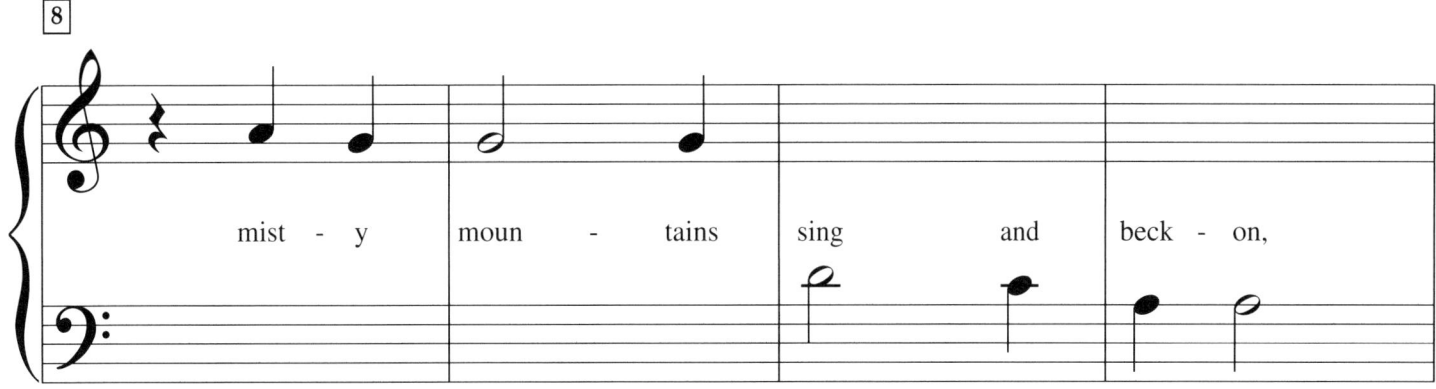
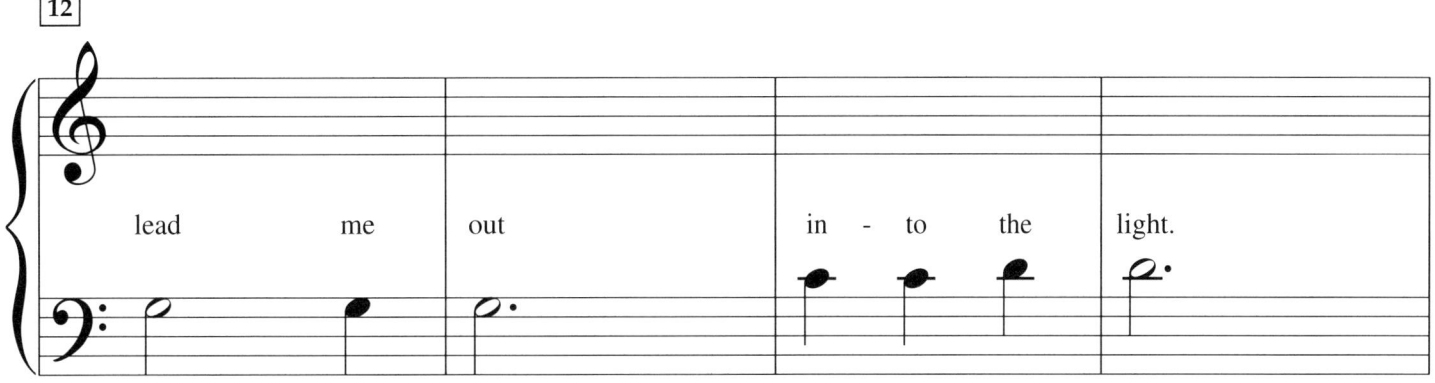
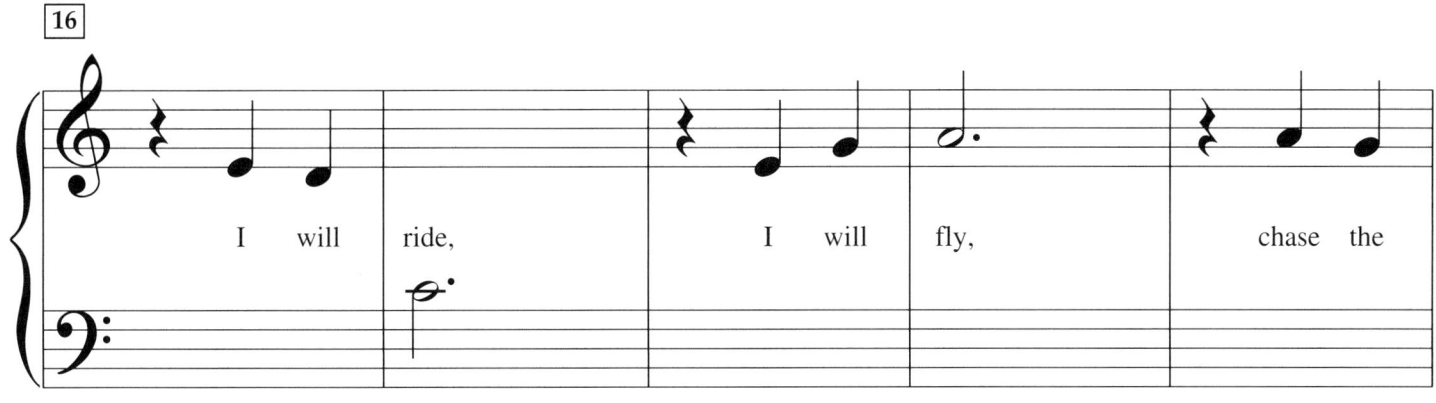
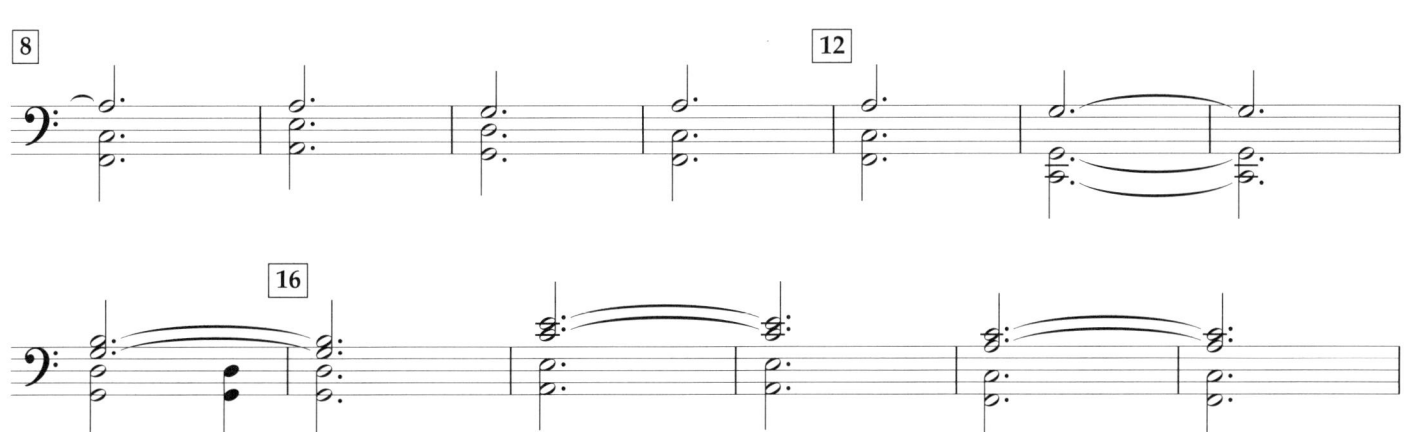

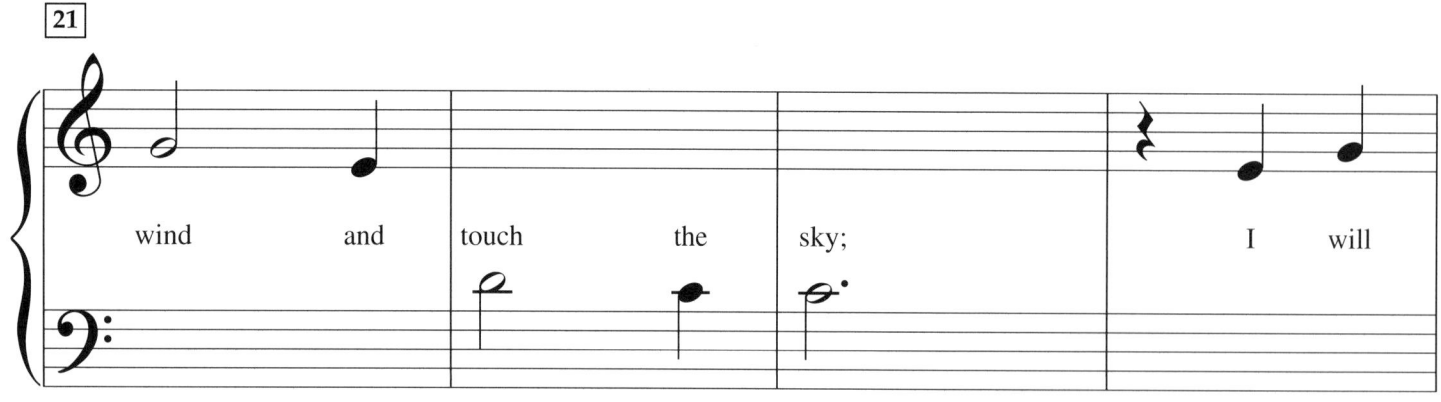

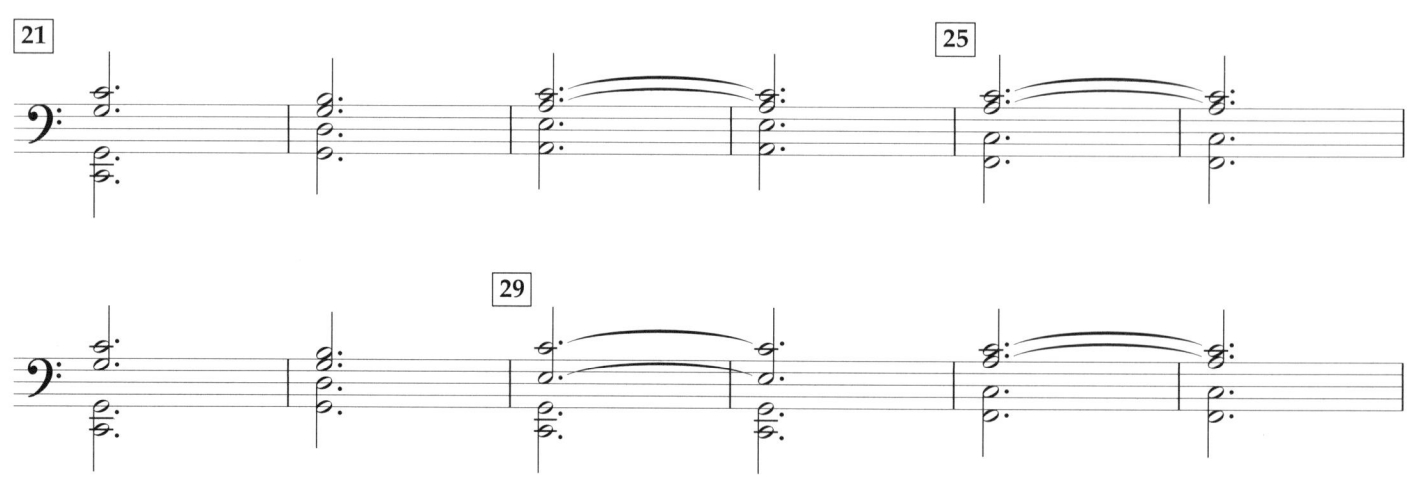

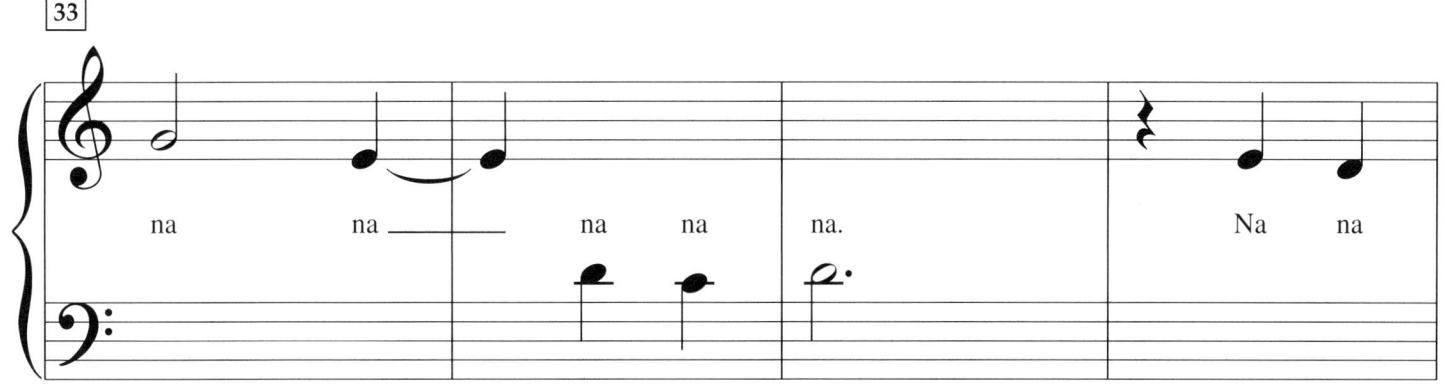
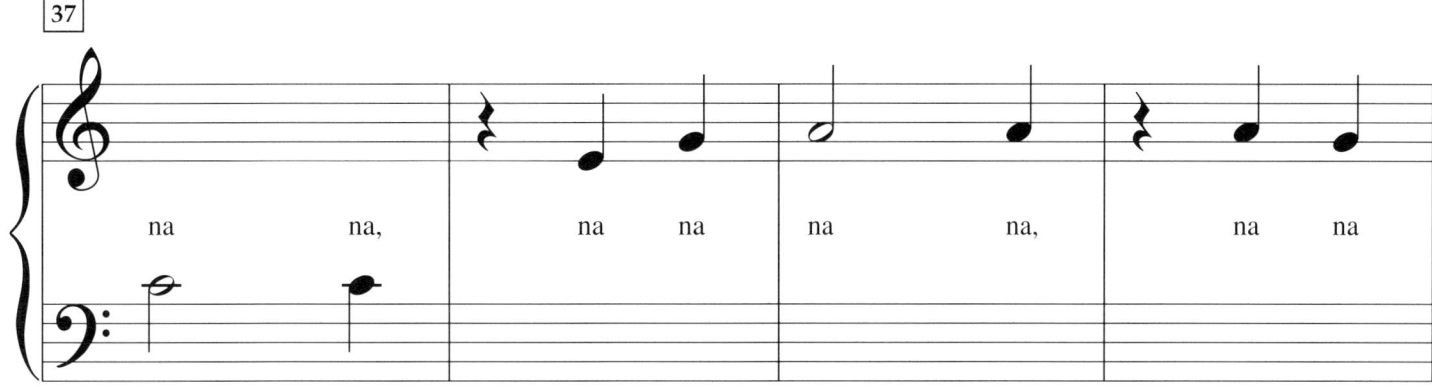
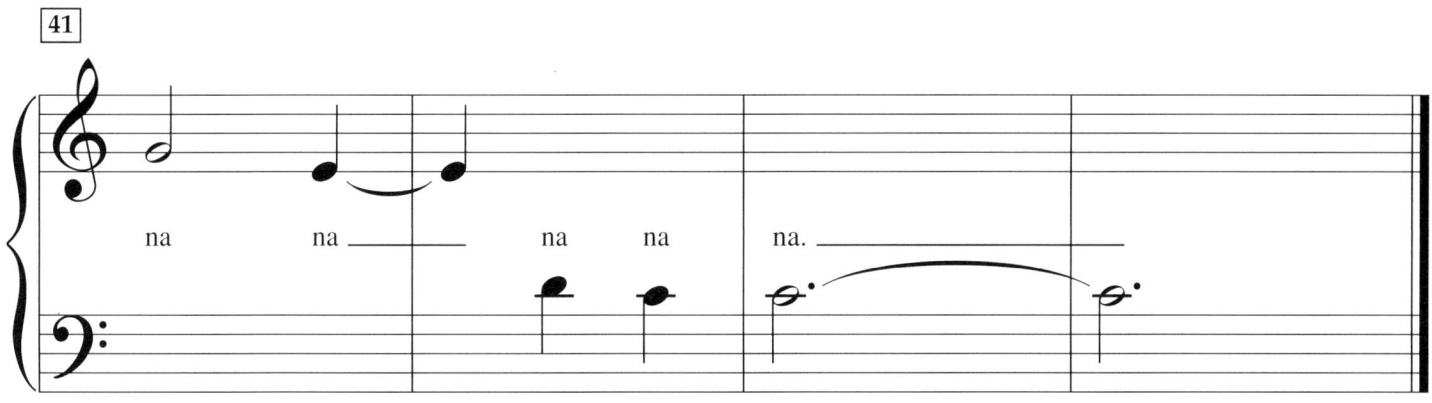
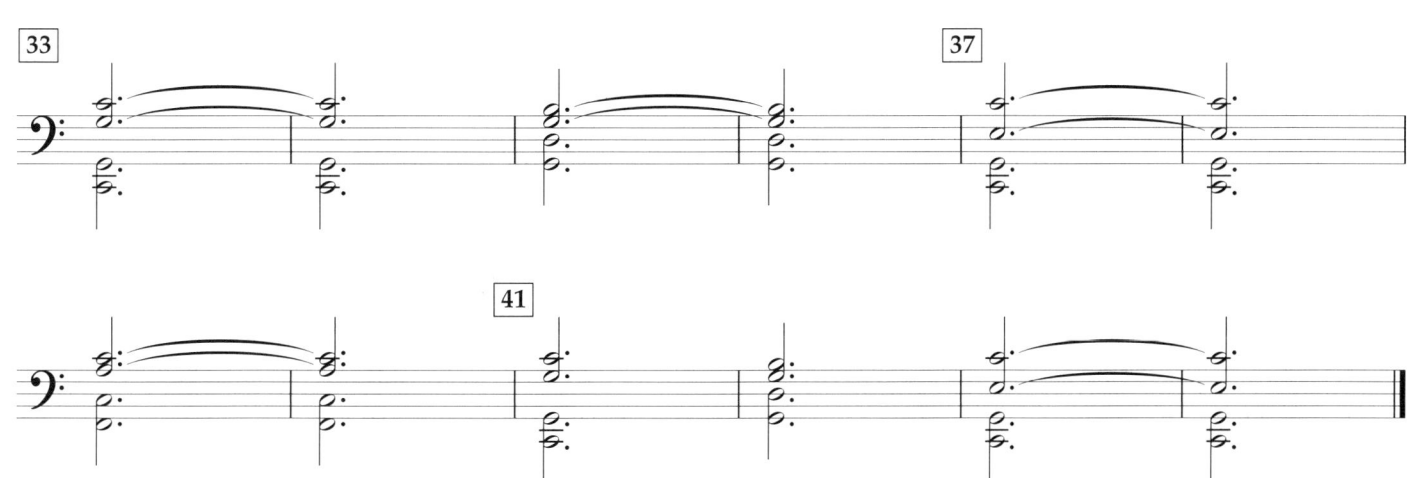

Scales and Arpeggios
from Walt Disney's THE ARISTOCATS

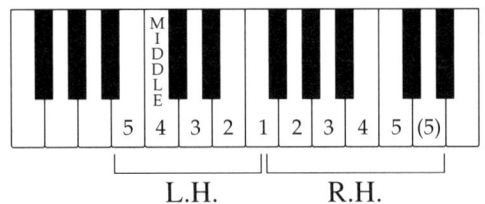

Words and Music by Richard M. Sherman
and Robert B. Sherman

Do mi so do do so mi do. Ev-'ry tru-ly cul-tured mu-sic
If you're faith-ful to your dai-ly
Though at first it seems as though it

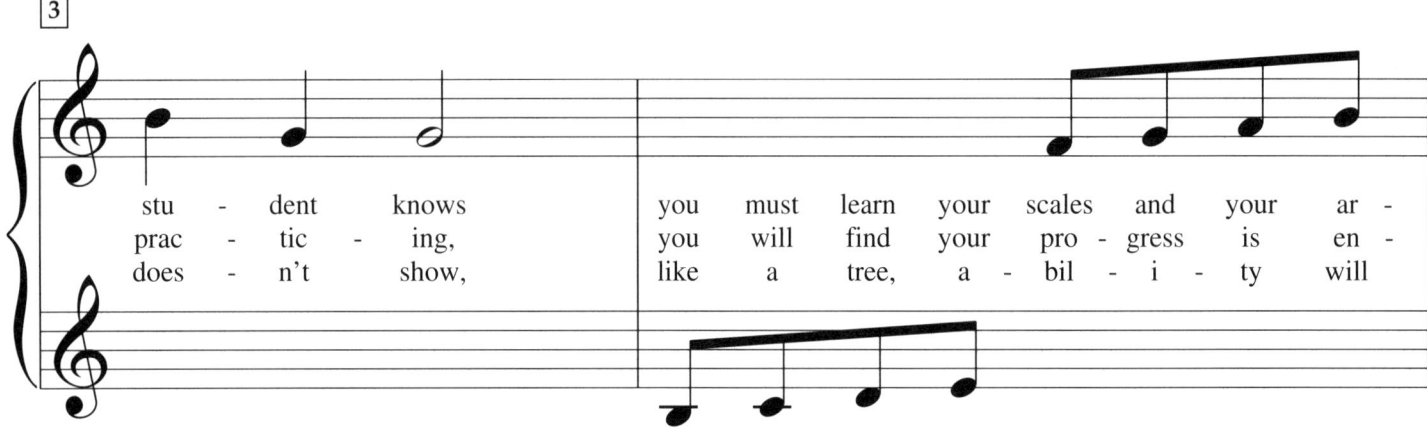

stu - dent knows you must learn your scales and your ar -
prac - tic - ing, you will find your pro - gress is en -
does - n't show, like a tree, a - bil - i - ty will

Duet Part (Student plays one octave higher than written.)

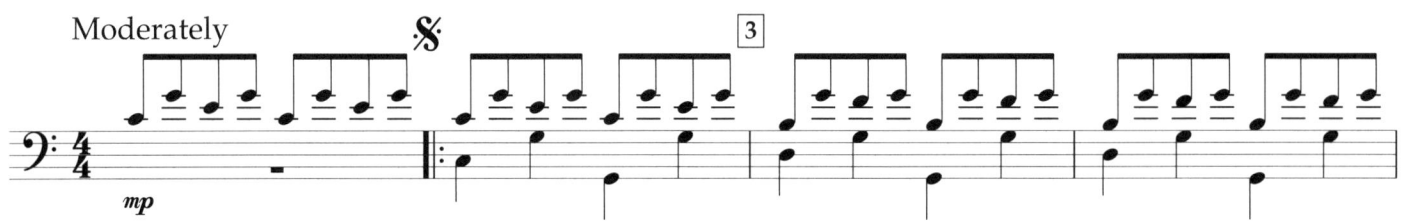

© 1968 Wonderland Music Company, Inc.
Copyright Renewed
All Rights Reserved Used by Permission

13
16
D.S. al Coda
Do mi so do do so mi do.
Do mi so do do so mi do.
CODA
(5)
5
peg - gi - os.
13
16
D.S. al Coda
CODA

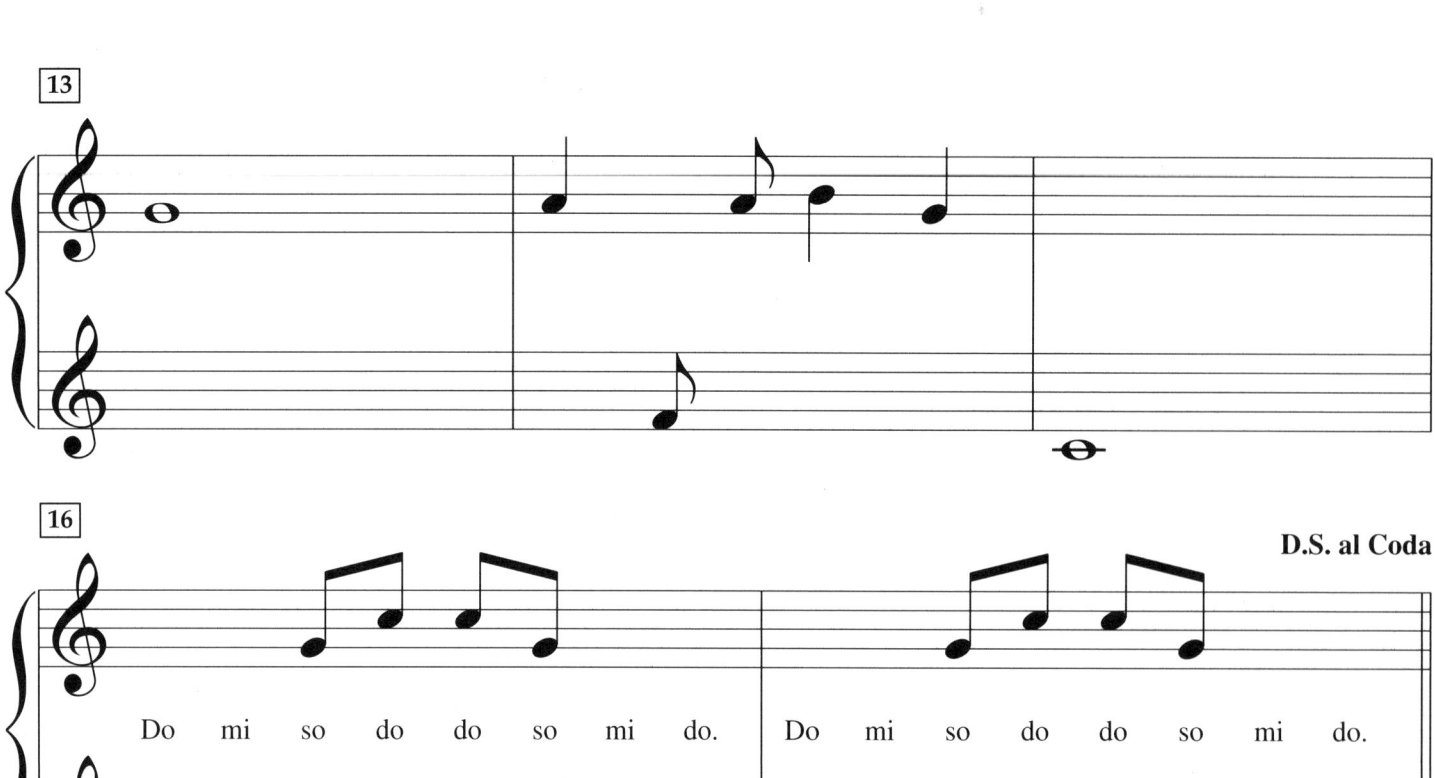

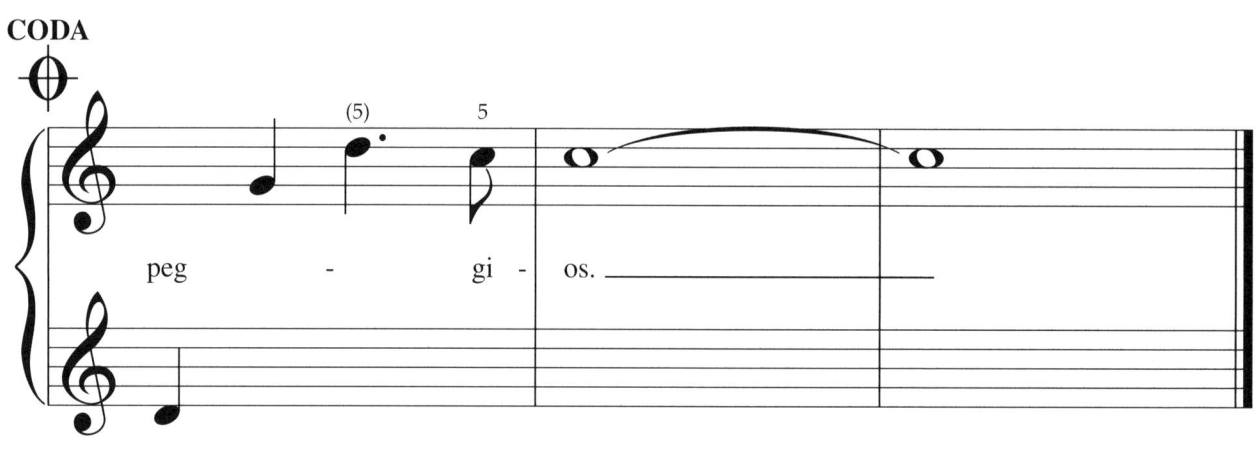

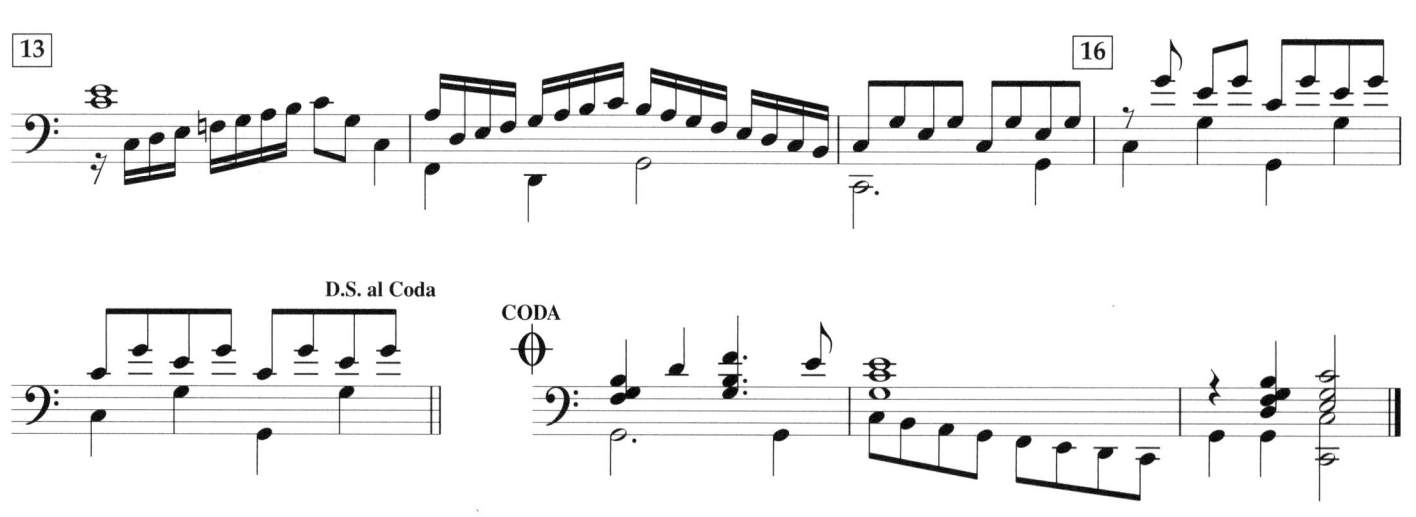